# TOURIST ATTRACTIONS IN SOUTH AFRICA

## *GUIDE BOOK*

ALI MOHAMMED

# DEDICATION

I dedicate this book to God for making it a success and also given me a life and good health to come up with this great product.

# CONTENTS

# INTRODUCTION

With Mandela's release in 1990 and the country's first democratic elections in 1994, things changed rapidly. South African Airways resumed flights to the U.S., Australia, and parts of Europe and expanded to new markets. Suddenly, all eyes were on the nation. "Many international visitors flocked to experience the new South Africa," says Mariette Du Toit-Helmbold, CEO of Cape Town Tourism from 2003-2013 and founder of destination-marketing agency Destination. "Tourism numbers saw a drastic increase during the 'post-apartheid honeymoon-phase.'"

Instead of brushing history under the rug, apartheid era relics were transformed into museums dedicated to telling the story of South Africa's turbulent road to democracy. The Apartheid Museum in Johannesburg and the District Six Museum in Cape Town recount personal experiences of lives affected during the regime, and former prisons were transformed into powerful museums like Constitution Hill and Robben Island, which remain major tourist destinations today. The safari industry also boomed, as more and more visitors descended to experience Kruger National Park and other game reserves.

The nation's first push to lure leisure travelers came with the historic 1995 Rugby World Cup, which marked South Africa's reentry onto the global sports stage after decades of pariah status. "We started fixing our airports, hotels, and basic road infrastructure that was the start of us capitalizing on that 15 minutes of fame," says Enver Duminy, current CEO of Cape Town Tourism and a member of the board of South Africa Tourism.

Hoping to ride the wave of positive coverage generated by the Rugby World Cup, Cape Town put in a failed bid for the 2004 Olympics. Given the challenges the young country was facing in overcoming the legacy of apartheid, there was rightfully much criticism over what many perceived as the government prioritizing investments in stadium and athletes over housing, education, and infrastructure. "That for us was also a realization that we had a long way to go," says Duminy.

Sports eventually brought South Africa to the forefront again, in the form of the 2010 FIFA World Cup. "That became the tipping point for

South Africa as being seen as a global destination," says Duminy. "The time was right for the destination to put its best face forward. We were in the households of millions of viewers who may have had the perception of South Africa having lions roaming around."

The country still reaps post-World Cup benefits such as improvements in roads, airports, and safety and security have transformed South Africa into a blue-chip destination. The country welcomed 10.8 million international tourists between May 2016 and May 2017 in 1988, by contrast, the county saw less than

400,000 foreign visitors. Today, tourism is the nation's fastestgrowing sector, for the first time in history surpassing mining as the biggest contributor to South Africa's GDP. Cape Town alone drew 1.7 million tourists between July 2016 and June 2017. Tourism boards have also been savvy about targeting new methods and markets. "It is no longer about the destination or your unique selling points; it is about the story," says Du Toit-Helmbold. "Our story is a complex one and is best told through local people."

South Africa continues to leverage its international spotlight by luring visitors with a diverse mix of offerings. The nation is home to a some of the continent's top luxury safari lodges, with a strong focus on conservation; the revitalization of Johannesburg's Central Business District is bringing visitors back to areas that were once a hotbed for crime; the opening of the Zeitz Museum of Contemporary Art Africa in a Thomas Heatherwick designed building in Cape Town is a boon for the continent's art community; and local chefs like Luke Dale-Roberts, whose Test Kitchen consistently makes appearances on world's best lists, are at the forefront of a vibrant culinary scene.

# TABLE MOUNTAIN NATIONAL PARK

Table Mountain is known for panoramic views over the city and the amazing coastline. There are numerous trails that allow hikers to explore around and atop the famous mountain. The majority of trails are rated moderate with some difficult trips to challenge the adventurous.

The summit occurs at 3,558 feet (1,084.6 m) which is not all that tall for a mountain. It is not the height but rather the unique presentation of a long flat top that serves as a backdrop for the city.

The plateau top of Table Mountain measures two miles (3 km) across from one end to the other. This plateau is nestled between Devil's Peak to the east and Lion's Head to the west.

The summit of the mountain may be reached either by a cable car or by hiking to the top for the more adventurous. Hiking up the mountain is one of the leading activities of those visiting the area.

Table Mountain is located at the northern end of the Cape Peninsula mountain range. The range runs from Cape Point in the south to Table Mountain in the north.

# CAPE OF GOOD HOPE

Cape of Good Hope is a rugged headland located on the southern tip of Cape Peninsula in South Africa. It sits on the Atlantic Ocean side of the peninsula. Most people find this landscape to rather remarkable and photogenic.

The oceanic meeting point occurs between Cape Agulhas and Cape Point which is 0.75 miles (1.2 km) east of the cape. The cape serves as a waypoint whether on the Cape Route or the Clipper Route.

# SUN CITY RESORT

History was made in 1979 when Sun City was opened in the North West to become the best holiday resort in South Africa, and for good reason.

Home to the Valley of Waves and sprawled along the border of the Pilanesberg National Park, Sun City Resort enjoys the fine distinction of being the only surf-and-safari destination within a two-hour drive of landlocked Johannesburg. Whether you're looking for a romantic stay with your partner, a fun weekend getaway with friends or a North West holiday with the whole family, Sun City Resort has it all.

Sun City is a luxury resort and casino, situated in the North West Province of South Africa. It is located between the Elands River and the Pilanesberg, about 140 km northwest of Johannesburg, near the city of Rustenburg. The complex borders the Pilanesberg National Park. It is made up of a number of themed sub-resorts with hotels on each, including the original Sun City Resort, The Cabanas, The Cascades and the Lost City (The Palace)

# KRUGER NATIONAL PARK

Kruger National Park is a South African National Park and one of the largest game reserves in Africa. It covers an area of 19,623 km2 (7,576 sq mi) in the provinces of Limpopo and Mpumalanga in northeastern South Africa, and extends 360 km (220 mi) from north to south and 65 km (40 mi) from east to west. The administrative headquarters are in Skukuza. Areas of the park were first protected by the government of the South African

Republic in 1898, and it became South Africa's first national park in 1926.

To the west and south of the Kruger National Park are the two South African provinces of Limpopo and Mpumalanga, respectively. To the north is Zimbabwe, and to the east is Mozambique. It is now part of the Great Limpopo Trans frontier Park, a peace park that links Kruger National Park with the Gonarezhou National Park in Zimbabwe, and with the Limpopo National Park in Mozambique.

The park is part of the Kruger to Canyons Biosphere, an area designated by the United Nations Educational, Scientific and Cultural

Organization (UNESCO) as an International Man and Biosphere Reserve.

The park has nine main gates allowing entrance to the different camps.

The park lies in the north-east of South Africa, in the eastern parts of Limpopo and Mpumalanga provinces . Phalaborwa, Limpopo is the only town in South Africa that borders the Kruger National Park. It is one of the largest national parks in the world, with an area of 19,485 km2 (7,523 sq mi). The park is approximately 360 km (220 mi) long, and has an average width of 65 km (40 mi). At its widest point, the park is 90 km (56 mi) wide from east to west. To the north and south of the park two rivers, the Limpopo and the Crocodile respectively, act as its natural boundaries. To the east the Lebombo Mountains separate it from Mozambique. Its western boundary runs parallel with this range, roughly 65 km (40 mi) distant. The park varies in altitude between 200 m (660 ft) in the east and 840 m (2,760 ft) in the south-west near Berg-en-Dal. The highest point in the park is here, a hill called Khandzalive. Several rivers run through the park from west to east, including the Sabie, Olifants, Crocodile, Letaba, L uvuvhu and Limpopo Rivers.

# CLIMATE

The climate of the Kruger National Park and lowveld is subtropical/tropical, specifically a hot semi-arid climate (Köppen BSh). Summer days are humid and hot. The rainy season is from September until May. The Kruger National Park website lists September and October as the driest periods, culminating in the beginning of the rainy season late in October. Because the park spans 360 kilometres or 220 miles from north to south, climate can vary throughout the park. Skukuza in the southern part of the park is about 2 to 3 °C (3.6 to 5.4 °F) cooler throughout the year than Pafuri in the north, with significantly more rainfall.

# VICTORIA AND ALFRED WATERFRONT

The Victoria & Alfred (V&A) Waterfront in Cape Town is situated on the Atlantic shore, Table Bay Harbour, the City of Cape Town and Table Mountain. Adrian van der Vyver designed the complex.

Situated in South Africa's oldest working harbour, the 123 hectares (300 acres) area has been developed for mixed-use, with both residential and commercial real estate.

The Waterfront attracts more than 23 million visitors a year.

# HISTORY

Prince Alfred, second son of Queen Victoria, visited the Cape Colony harbour in 1860 as a sixteen-year-old Royal Navy Midshipman on HMS Euryalus. He made a big splash with the colonials on this first-ever visit by a member of the Royal Family. The first basin of the new Navy Yard was named after him and the second after his mother.

On the 25 August 1998 the Planet Hollywood bombing took place at the (now closed) Planet Hollywood restaurant within the V&A killing 2 people and injuring 26 more

The Waterfront has seen development in its new Silo district, which currently houses the new headquarters of Allan

Gray Investment Management at Silo 1 and apartments at Silo 2. The project was completed in 2017 with a Virgin Active gym, the Zeitz Museum of Contemporary Art Africa, and the adjoining ultra-luxury Silo Hotel.

# HLUHLUWE– IMFOLOZI PARK

Hluhluwe Imfolozi Park, formerly Hluhluwe Umfolozi Game Reserve, is the oldest proclaimed nature reserve in Africa. It consists of 960 km² (96,000 ha) of hilly topography 280 kilometers (170 mi) north of Durban in central KwaZulu Natal, South Africa and is known for its rich wildlife and conservation efforts. Operated by Ezemvelo KZN Wildlife, the park is the only state-run park in KwaZulu Natal where each of the big five game animals can be found.

Thanks to conservation efforts, the park now has one of the largest populations of white rhinoceros in the world.

## HISTORY

Throughout the park there are many signs of Stone Age settlements and iron smelting sites. The area is claimed to have been declared a royal hunting ground for the Zulu kingdom in the time of Shaka.

The southern white rhino, first identified by Western naturalist William John Burchell in 1812, was virtually eliminated during the 19th century by European hunters, and by 1895 was believed to be extinct. A population of between 20 and 100 was identified in South Africa and preserved by establishing the Umfolozi Junction Reserve and Hluhluwe Reserve, which are now parts of the Hluhluwe-Imfolozi Park.

Historically, tsetse flies carrying the nagana disease protected the area from colonial hunters. Later, as the Zululand area was settled by white farmers, wildlife in the reserves was blamed for the prevalence of the tsetse fly, and the reserves became experimental areas in the efforts to eradicate the fly. Farmers called for the slaughter of game and over 100,000 animals were killed in the reserves between 1919 and 1950, although the rhino population was spared. The introduction of DDT spraying in 1945 virtually eliminated the tsetse fly from the reserves, although subsequent outbreaks have occurred.

By the 1950s the white rhino population of the reserve had recovered to around 400, and the park's warden, Ian Player, established Operation Rhino in the 1950s and 60s, with the park's Rhino Capture Unit relocating hundreds of rhinos to establish populations in other reserves across their historic range.

In 1989, the corridor between the Hluhluwe and Imfolozi reserves was added in order to join the separate reserves into the current single park.

The park is located in the province of KwaZulu Natal on the east coast of South Africa. The park is closest to the town of Mtubatuba,

Hluhluwe village and Hlabisa village. The geography of the area differs from the north, or Hluhluwe area, to the south, or Umfolozi area. Hluhluwe Imfolozi Park is partly in a low-risk malaria area.

This area is situated between the two Umfolozi Rivers where they divide into the Mfolozi emnyama ('Black Umfolozi') to the north and the Mfolozi emhlophe ('White Umfolozi') to the south. This area is to the south of the park and is generally hot in summer, and mild to cool in winter, although cold spells do occur. The topography in the Umfolozi section ranges from the lowlands of the Umfolozi River beds to steep hilly country, which includes some wide and deep valleys. Habitats

Rhinos grazing in the Park

The park is the birthplace of rhino preservation, having been responsible for breeding the southern white rhinoceros back from near extinction in the first half of the 20th century. There are reportedly 1,600 white rhino in the reserve.

The rhino population remains severely threatened by the increase in rhino poaching within the park and elsewhere, with 222 rhinos poached in the province in 2017, most of them in the park. On 6 March 2020 two of three suspected rhino poachers were killed in a shootout, after an infrared camera automatically alerted the operations centre, providing number of persons, grid reference and direction of the incursion. Hluhluwe–Imfolozi has implemented Smart Park which facilitates the integration of systems, including drone technology, for early detection and rapid response of reaction units.

## AFRICAN WILD DOG

In 1981, the Natal Parks board (now Ezemvelo KZN Wildlife) attempted to reintroduce African wild dogs into the park. Twenty-three dogs were released in the reserve, most of which had been bred in zoos. However this met with limited success and by 2015, the population had fluctuated between 3 and 30 individuals. Further dogs were released into the park in 2022.

The first visitor camp was built at Hilltop in 1934, and is now the main camp in the northern (Hluhluwe) section of the park. The main camp in the southern (Umfolozi) section is Mpila. The reserve has a 300-kilometre (190 mi) road network.

# BLYDE RIVER CANYON

The Blyde River Canyon is a 26km long Canyon located in Mpumalanga, South Africa. It is the one of the larger canyons on Earth but much smaller than those of Asia, the Grand Canyon and the Fish River Canyon. Unlike the Grand and Fish River Canyon, the Blyde River Canyon is a "green canyon" which is dominated by subtropical vegetation. The canyon forms part of the Blyde River Canyon Nature Reserve.

The Blyde River Canyon passes a rock formation known as the "Three Rondavels". So named as the formation resembles three African-style houses or rondavels. This canyon is part of the Panorama Route. This route starts at the town Graskop and includes God's Window, the Pinnacle and Bourke's Luck Potholes.

The Blyde River Canyon

The canyon is named for the river that runs through it, the Blyde River, now called the Motlatse River. Blyde means "glad" or "happy" in Old Dutch, a name derived from a voortrekkers' expedition. The 'happy river' was thus named in 1844, when Hendrik Potgieter and others returned safely from Delagoa Bay to the rest of their party of trekkers who had considered them dead. While still under this misapprehension they had named the nearby river where they had been encamped, Treurrivier, or 'mourning river'.

In 2005, the Blyde River was renamed to the Motlatse River, and the Mpumalanga Provincial Government announced that the canyon would be renamed as well. (clarification needed)

The Blyde as it exits the canyon near Swadeni

The Blyde River Canyon supports large diversity of life, including numerous fish and antelope species as well as hippos and crocodiles, and every primate species that may be seen in South Africa (including both greater and lesser bushbabies, ver vet monkeys and Samango monkeys).

The diversity of birdlife is similarly high, including the beautiful and much sought Narina trogon as well as species such as the Cape vulture, black eagle, crowned eagle, African fish eagle, gymnogene, jackal buzzard, white-rumped vulture, bald ibis, African finfoot, Knysna lourie, purple-crested lourie, Gurney's sugarbird, malachite sunbird, cinnamon dove, African emerald cuckoo, redbacked mannikin, golden-tailed woodpecker, olive bush shrike, green twinspot, Taita falcons (very rarely sighted, a breeding pair lives in the nearby Abel Erasmus Pass), Cape eagle owl, white-faced owl, wood owl, peregrine falcon, black-breasted snake eagle, Wahlberg's eagle, longcrested eagle, lanner falcon, redbreasted sparrowhawk, rock kestrel and others.

The upper canyon as seen from Bourke's Luck at the TreurBlyde confluence

At 200 metres (660 ft), the Kadishi Tufa waterfall is the second tallest tufa waterfall on earth. A tufa waterfall is formed when water running over dolomite rock absorbs calcium, and deposits rock formations more rapidly than they erode the surrounding rock. In the case of the Kadishi Tufa fall, the formation that has been produced strikingly resembles a face which is crying profusely, and is thus sometimes known as 'the weeping face of nature'.

## Tourism

The Three Rondavels in the Blyde River Canyon

The canyon and the surrounding Drakensberg escarpment i s a very popular tourist region with a well-developed tourism industry supported by good public infrastructure.

# WINE-TASTING IN CAPE TOWN

Wine tasting is one of the best ways to spend a day in Cape Town. Combine the delicious wines with some of the most beautiful landscapes on earth, century old architecture, and awe-inspiring food, and it's no surprise that it's one of Cape Town's most beloved activities for visitors and locals alike.

Wine estates are a dime a dozen, so it can be hard to know where to start. Take a look at our guide to wine-tasting in Cape Town and get ready to enjoy the finest wines of the region!

For discounts and free entry to loads of

Cape Town's top attractions, get your City Pass now!

The Constantia Wine Route

The Constantia Wine Route is no more than 20 minutes away from the city. The magnificent landscape is home to some of the country's oldest and most prestigious wine farms dating back to the 1650s. The wines of the Constantia Vineyards are largely cool climate offerings, so look out for world class sauvignon blancs, delightful reds and the famous Constantia dessert wine.

## THE STELLENBOSCH WINE ROUTE

Boasting nearly 200 wine and grape producers, Stellenbosch was the first region to establish a formal route among the wineries a route which has gone on to become one of the country's six most popular tourist destinations. 148 wine farms adorn the vine-covered landscape, many of them historical farms with achingly beautiful Cape Dutch manors houses, gardens, hotels, and fine-dining restaurants.

## THE HELDERBERG WINE ROUTE

The wineries that fall within the Helderberg Wine Route are all in and around the Somerset West area, a 30 minute drive from the city. Historic estates line up alongside cutting edge modern cellars, all producing a wonderful diverse array of wines. In recent times, it has acquired a reputation for producing impressive white wines, particularly sauvignon blanc and chardonnay.

## THE DURBANVILLE WINE ROUTE

A short drive 20 minute drive north of the city is all it takes to experience wonderful wine and dine parings at any number of the Durbanville estates. One of the region's many virtues is also the spectacular views back across the ocean towards Table Mountain. You can also dip your toes in the rivers of the nearby nature reserve on a pretty morning. The region creates intense, fruit-driven yet refined wines, as unique as the slopes they grew on and the master wine makers who crafted them.

## THE FRANSCHHOEK WINE ROUTE

Franschhoek is another wine route with outrageously beautiful landscapes. With many of the wine farms sharing a French Huguenot heritage, expect to find enormous French influence here.

The Champagne-inspired sparkling "Cap Classique" is the star of this show. The gorgeously quaint village of Franschhoek abounds with art galleries, antique shops, restaurants and boutique hotels. Take the Wine Tram for a lovely bit of history.

# KNYSNA

Knysna is a town with 76,150 inhabitants (2019 mid-year estimates) in the Western Cape province of South Africa. and is one of the destinations on the loosely defined Garden Route tourist route. It lies at 34° 2' 6.3168'' S and 23° 2' 47.2884'' E., and is situated 60 kilometers east of the city of George on the N2 highway, and 33 kilometres west of the Plettenberg Bay on the same road.

## HISTORY

Forty fossilised hominid footprints, dating to about 90,000 years ago, along with various other archaeological discoveries suggest that humans have lived in Knysna for well over 300,000 years. The first of these were various San Hunter-gatherer peoples who inhabited most of Southern Africa in paleolithic. The San were gradually displaced and absorbed by south migrating Khoekhoe peoples.

The indigenous inhabitants of the Knysna area are a southern Khoekhoe people called the Houtunqua or Outeniqua. Their name means "The People Who Bear Honey". From the Khoekhoegowab words '/hao 'hone y', tun'(teni) verb 'to carry', and khoe rendered as qua meaning 'people'.

Little is known about Houtunqua society prior to European contact.

What little historical sources exist are not elaborate. It is suspected that at the height of the Houtunqua's society territory stretched from the mouth of the Krom River in the east, along the Outeniqua Mountains which bear their name, up until the mouth of the Grootbrak River in the west.

KHOEKHOE HUNTERS.

The Houtunqua seem to have remained autonomous from the Inqua (Hamcumqua) expansion in the north with smaller Khoekhoe tribes like the Gamtobaqua coming into the fold of the Houtunqua to seek protection from the ever expanding Inqua to the north east. The Houtunqua were connected to trades routes with the Attaqua and Hessequa to the west.

Archaeological evidence suggests that the Houtunqua kept livestock and practiced Nomadic Pastoralism but made extensive use of the resources in mountain forests. Excavations in the region have unearthed many caves showing signs of pre-colonial occupation.The discovery of shell middens at Knoetzie beach confirms the idea that like other Khoekhoe peoples, the Houtuniqua made use of the ocean for its resources.

Oral tradition among the Houtunqua tells how the Houtunqua held specific superstitions about Europeans and believed them to be "baleful spirits".

Thus the Houtunqua went out of their way to avoid contact with Europeans. Where other Khoekhoe tribes established formal relations and trade with Europeans, the Houtunqua receded deeper and deeper into the mountain forests. As a result the Houtunqua disappeared from the historical record for some time with some Houtunqua eventually assimilating into colonial society of the time. Chief Dikkop, who died in 1816, was the last recorded Chief of the Houtunqua.

## ORIGINS OF THE NAME

A number of explanations exist for the origins of the name, 'Knysna' including 'xthys xna,' purportedly from a

Khoekhoe language term that night mean have meant 'place of timber', 'place of ferns', or even 'straight down' (referring to the cliffs at The Heads). However, it is also likely that the name is related to, or a derivative of, similar place names that do or have existed in other parts of Africa. In colonial times Lake Malawi was known as Lake Nyasa (very similar to 'Knysna'), while Webster's Universal Unabridged Dictionary defines the word 'nyanza' as a noun `"(African): An expanse of water, as a lake or wide river".

EUROPEAN SETTLEMENT

The SS Agnar tows an unknown sailing ship into Knysna Harbour in 1910.

The first Europeans arrived in the area in 1760, and the farm Melkhoutkraal (literally translating from Afrikaans as 'milk wood kraal') was established on the eastern shore of the Knysna Lagoon. Stephanus Terblans, the first European farmer to settle in the area, was given a loan permit to farm here in 1770.

Upon moving to Knysna George Rex, a British-born entrepreneur credited as being the founder of Knysna, acquired the loan rights to Melkhoutkraal in 1804 and later, in 1816, to the farm Welbedacht, which he renamed Eastford. He gave 80 acres (32 ha) of Eastford to the Colonial

Government, on which the Royal Navy established the township of Melville. Rex's properties were sold when he died in 1839.

In April 1817, the transport brig Emu, belonging to the Cape Town Dockyard, was the first European vessel to enter the Knysna heads. She struck a rock, now known as Emu Rock, and was holed. Her crew ran Emu ashore to prevent her sinking. In late April HMS Podargus arrived to render assistance. After surveying the area, Podargus sailed safely into the Knysna and retrieved Emu's cargo.

The next major settler in Knysna was Captain Thomas Henry Duthie, who married Caroline, George Rex's daughter, and bought a portion of the

Uitzigt farm from his father-in-law which Rex had named Belvidere. The construction of a small Norman-style church was commissioned by Duthie on his property, and was consecrated in 1855. The settlement's population grew slowly, and Englishmen such as Henry Barrington and Lt. Col. John Sutherland, who established the settlement of Newhaven on a portion of purchased land, settled in the area. At the time, Knysna was a field cornetcy of Plettenberg Bay within the Magisterial Division of George. In 1858, Knysna became a separate Magisterial Division, new stores and accommodation facilities were opened, and Knysna became the new commercial centre of the region.

On their way to New Zealand, the Thesen family who were travelling from Norway fancied the little hamlet of Knysna so much that they decided to stay, bringing with them their knowledge of commerce and sailing.

Soon, timber was being exported to the Cape from the vast areas of forest surrounding Knysna, and a steam sawmill and small shipyard were established. Later, these were relocated to Paarden Island, later known as Thesen's Island.

In 1878, an important discovery was made in the area. A gold nugget was found in the Karatara River, near Ruigtevlei. Soon fortune hunters from all over the world arrived at the Millwood Forest in search of gold, and Millwood grew into a bustling town.

Millwood was declared a gold field, the first in South Africa. However, soon not enough gold was being recovered to sustain a growing town, and the mining industry in the area collapsed. Some miners relocated to Knysna, bringing their little homes with them. One of the houses, known as 'Millwood House', now functions as a museum.

# AMALGAMATION AND TIMBER INDUSTRY

By 1880 over 1000 people had settled in Knysna. In 1882, the settlements of Newhaven, Melville and the "wedge" of land between the two villages were amalgamated to form the municipality of 'The Knysna', named after the Knysna River.

Knysna's timber industry peaked when George Parkes arrived from Britain and saw the opportunity to use the hardwoods of the Knysna Forest for export to elsewhere in the country, and even overseas. He established the Knysna Forest Company, later renamed Geo.

Parkes and Sons Ltd., which is still trading to this day.

## 2017 KNYSNA FIRE

On June 7, 2017, fueled by strong winds from a severe storm - the Cape Storm of 2017 coming in from the west, a fire swept through the town and surrounding areas. Killing 9 as a direct result of the fires and another 2 indirectly and displacing around 10,000 people from all walks of life. Initially reported as arson, the cause of the fire was later revealed to have been arson.

The town is primarily built on the northern shore of a large warmwater estuary, known as the Knysna Lagoon, which is fed by the Knysna River. The estuary opens to the ocean after passing between two large headlands made up of Peninsula Formation quartzites. These are popularly known as "The Heads", and have become infamous due to the loss of boats and fishermen passing through their treacherous and unpredictable waters.

The Paquita, a German vessel, sank on the eastern side of the Knysna Heads in 1903. Near them are geological formations, known locally as "The Map Stones." To the north of Knysna, AfroMontane or temperate rainforest covers the hilly terrain for 20 km until changing to fynbos or macchia high in the Outeniqua Mountains.

# DURBAN BEACHES

They don't call Durban "South Africa's Playground" for nothing. It is South Africa's very own seaside paradise, famous for its beaches and the warm Indian Ocean. So dig your toes in the sand, take a dip in the sea and enjoy your time in South Africa's third biggest city.

Durban's beaches lie along a stretch of golden sand, known locally as the Golden Mile. From Blue Lagoon's fishing spot to the sunken Vetch's Pier, a host of flat, sandy beaches invite you to set down an umbrella and towel, and while away hours in the sun.

Blessed with warm water, robust waves and seemingly endless stretches of sandy beaches, you'll soon understand why

Durban (eThekwini) is everyone's favourite seaside playground. Warm and sunny most of the year year, Durban's beaches offer public amenities, protective shark nets, beacons to indicate safe bathing and lifeguards on duty for most of the day.

Sunshine, sand, rock pools and warm water typify the idyllic beach conditions at Umdloti; while Addington Beach, close to the harbour entrance at the southern end of Durban Bay, is more protected, which means smaller waves that lend itself to learning how to surf. Durban's South Beach is a popular surf spot and is known as a safe place for beginner surfers. North Beach delivers stunning sunrise's all year round and is blissfully warm. Then there is Dairy Beach on Durban's Golden Mile, which is a renowned surfing spot.

About 15 minutes' north of Durban, Umhlanga Rocks beach is lined with luxury hotels and apartments. This is a fun spot with a permanent holiday vibe. Umhlanga's village is full of restaurants, sidewalk cafes, pubs and clubs. If you're after a quieter spot, Umhlanga's Bronze Beach is more secluded, while Umdloti, Salt Rock and Zinkwazi, further north, are more family friendly.

Down the South Coast you'll find a selection of pristine Blue Flag beaches including Hibberdene, Margate, Marina, Umzumbe, Ramsgate, Lucien and Trafalgar.

For some of the most pristine stretches of sand in the world, places like Kosi Bay, Cape Vidal and Sodwana Bay (part of the iSimangaliso Wetlands Park World Heritage Site) offer unspoilt beaches and plentiful fauna and flora. Sodwana has the added bonus of being the prime diving spot in South Africa, sometimes referred to as "South Africa's Barrier Reef".

Durban boasts 600km of subtropical beaches on its coastline and what makes this fantastic coastline even better is that the area has fantastic weather all year round even in winter. The people are friendly and there is no greater place to enjoy a vibrant beach holiday anywhere else in the world.

# West Coast National Park

The West Coast National Park lies 88 km (55 mi) north of Cape Town in the Western Cape province of South Africa. The park is found inside of the Cape West Coast Biosphere Reserve, part of the UNESCO Man and the Biosphere Programme. It is bordered by the Atlantic Ocean on the west and the R27 coastal road, and runs from the town of Yzerfontein in the south, up to the Langebaan Lagoon. The park is particularly well known for its bird life and for the spring flowers which occur in the months from August to September, especially in the Postberg flower reserve section of the park. The park, with the islands in Saldanha Bay, has been identified by BirdLife International as an Important Bird Area. The park was proclaimed in 1985, and is 36,259.8 hectares (140.000 sq mi) in size.

## HISTORY OF PROTECTION

The Langebaan Lagoon, a Ramsar site, was proclaimed as a marine reserve in 1973. Concerns over the condition of the Langebaan Lagoon and neighbouring Saldanha Bay led to a proposal in 1976 that the Langebaan Lagoon, the peninsula, the offshore islands and the surrounding land urgently be proclaimed as a nature reserve. The Langebaan National Park was declared in 1985, after a long process, and it was expanded in 1987 when some land which had been managed by the Department of Forestry and neighboring farms were included in the park. In that same year an additional 1,800 hectares (4,400 acres) of land around Postberg was included as a "contractual national park". Expansion has continued since then. Its name was changed to West Coast National Park in 1987. In 2000, the park and Langebaan Lagoon was added to the UNESCO Cape West Coast Biosphere Reserve.

Wildlife in the park includes

large antelope such as eland, red hartebeest, bontebok, kudu, gemsbok, steenbok, mountain
zebra, duiker and ostriches in the Postberg section. Other smaller

animals include the bat-eared fox, caracal, and Cape gray mongoose.

Many Palearctic migrants winter in the lagoon during the austral summer, particularly in September as species arrive from the northern hemisphere, and in March when they gather in large numbers to feed up prior to undertaking the return migration. At these times the birds will be transitioning out of and into their breeding plumage. The birds are pushed towards the hides as the water level rises with the tide and eventually they must fly off until the tide has receded once more. Red knot, sanderling, little stint, Ruff, marsh, Terek and Curlew sandpipers, ruddy turnstone, ringed and grey plover, greenshank, Eurasian whimbrel,

Eurasian curlew and bartailed godwit are the most regular species. Little egret and South African shelduck are resident and can often be seen with the waders, while greater flamingoes and great white pelican occur in deeper water. An isolated hide west of the Geelbek educational centre overlooks a salt pan where it is possible to observe the rare chestnut-banded plover. The lagoon's importance for migratory birds means that it is a site which is subject to the Ramsar Convention for the conservation and sustainable use of wetlands.

On the land, the fynbos surrounding the lagoon is home to southern black korhaan, Cape spurfowl and greywinged francolin, Cape penduline and grey tit, southern anteater chat, whitethroated and yellow canary, Karoo lark, chestnut-vented warbler, bokmakierie and Cape bunting, which are all easily seen. African marsh harrier and black Harrier hunt by quartering the ground. The coastal islands at the mouth of the lagoon are important breeding colonies for Cape and Hartlaub's gull, Cape gannet and African penguin, as well as cormorants and terns.

Although the thousands of migrating birds are an important part of the conservation, the flowers are also a major attraction. The park is composed of various kinds of habitats as well as the

Langebaan fynbos and lagoon which account for the variety of flora and fauna all around the park. The months of August and September bring about the proliferation of annual spring flowers in the West Coast National Park. During the spring flower season large fields of blooming White rain daisies (Dimorphotheca pluvialis), Gousblom (Arctotis hirsuta), Magriet (Ursinia anthemoides), Livingstone daisies (Dorotheanthus bellidiformis), and Wild sorrel (Oxalis pes-caprae) can be seen along with other species of flowing plants.

# Golden Gate Highlands National Park

Golden Gate Highlands National Park is located in the central part of western South Africa. It is in Free State, South Africa just north of Lesotho. The park covers an area of 130 square miles (340 sq km).

QwaQwa National Park became part of Golden Gate Highlands in 2004 creating one park for the combined larger area. The park is located in the Maluti Mountains with the Caledon River serving as the southern border of the park.

Ribbokkop is the highest summit in the national park reaching a height of 9,281 feet (2,829 m). The majority of vegetation is comprised of either Highveld or montane grasslands. Other vegetation includes Afromontane forest and the ouhout with the latter being the most prevalent.

The park is not known for its wildlife; however, it is there. Blesbok, eland, reedbuck, oribi, wildebeest, springbok, and zebra take advantage of the grasslands for grazing. They roam freely in the park which is void of any real predators.

There are over 210 species of birds that either nest or migrate through the park.  Bearded and Cape vultures along with the Verreaux's eagle are some of the larger species. There are poisonous snakes including the puff adder and the mountain adder that people should watch for as they explore the area.

The park is more renowned for the pristine wilderness and the landscapes created by the beautiful sandstone cliffs and fellow rock outcrops.

The national park is not known for its wildlife, however, that can be an added bonus to those taking in the landscape. The magnificent rock cropping and astounding sandstone cliffs are the highlights of the landscape.

The name of the park was generated by the sandstone cliffs that frame the valley. The sandstone cliffs display and variegated orange and yellow colors across their rock faces that are scattered throughout the park.

Rockcrops blanket the area and combine with the cliffs to create striking panoramic landscapes. Exploration of the landscapes has also led to discoveries of dinosaur remains. This adds to the historical significance of the terrain.

One of the best ways to experience the national park is through scenic drives that traverse the remarkable landscapes with a variety of vistas and panoramic views. There are hiking trails that allow travelers to engage the splendor of these endless rolling hills blanketed with beautiful sandstone cliffs and rock formations.

# Marakele National Park

The park is accessible to all passenger vehicles, with the camp and tent sites on good roads. Also, approximately 80 km of roads within the park are accessible to all vehicles, the balance requiring a four-wheel drive vehicle. Marakele is home to the big five (buffalo did not exist in the park, but 20 disease-free buffalo (nine cows and eleven bulls) were re-introduced on 15 October 2013) as well as sixteen species of antelopes and over 250 species of birds, including the largest colony of Cape griffon vultures in the world (around 800 breeding pairs). The Matlabas River runs through the park.

## HISTORY

The area now constituting Marakele was home to several iron-age settlements which are not yet open to public viewing. Prior to its foundation as a National Park, it was home to naturalist Eugene Marais. Marakele was founded as Kransberg National Park in 1994 with the purchase of 150 square kilometres (58 sq mi), and was shortly after renamed to its current name. By 1999, the park had expanded to 670 square kilometres (260 sq mi).

## ACCOMMODATION

Two tented camps are laid on in

Marakele, namely Tlopi and Bontle. The SANParks webpage informs that between April and September 2013, eight new tented units will be constructed at Bontle camp, but that the camping sites will be kept open for visitors.

# CONCLUSION

THANKS FOR READING THROUGH AND I HOPE YOU ENJOYED IT

# ABOUT THE AUTHOR

EMAIL: aarasheedmohammed@gmail.com

www.ingramcontent.com/pod-product-compliance
Lightning Source LLC
Chambersburg PA
CBHW071028220526
45467CB00004B/1557